INTRODUCTION TO OPEN TERRARIUM FOR DAVALLIA (RABBIT'S FOOT FERN) 4

BEAUTY OF OPEN TERRARIUM: A WINDOW INTO MINIATURE LANDSCAPES 6

CHOOSING THE RIGHT CONTAINER FOR DAVALLIA (RABBIT'S FOOT FERN) 9

ESSENTIAL TOOLS AND MATERIALS FOR DAVALLIA (RABBIT'S FOOT FERN) TERRARIUM 12

SOIL AND SUBSTRATE FOR DAVALLIA (RABBIT'S FOOT FERN) TERRARIUM 15

LIGHT REQUIREMENTS FOR DAVALLIA (RABBIT'S FOOT FERN) 18

TEMPERATURE CONSIDERATIONS FOR DAVALLIA (RABBIT'S FOOT FERN) 21

STEP-BY-STEP GUIDE TO BUILDING YOUR OPEN TERRARIUM FOR DAVALLIA (RABBIT'S FOOT FERN) 23

PREPARING THE CONTAINER FOR DAVALLIA (RABBIT'S FOOT FERN) TERRARIUM 26

PREPARING THE BASE LAYER OF YOUR OPEN TERRARIUM FOR DAVALLIA (RABBIT'S FOOT FERN) 29

ADDING THE GROWING MEDIUM AND OPTIMIZING SOIL CONDITIONS FOR DAVALLIA (RABBIT'S FOOT FERN) 31

ARRANGING DAVALLIA (RABBIT'S FOOT FERN) IN YOUR OPEN TERRARIUM 34

PROPER DRAINAGE TECHNIQUES FOR DAVALLIA (RABBIT'S FOOT FERN) IN OPEN TERRARIUMS 37

WATERING TECHNIQUES AND MAINTAINING PROPER MOISTURE LEVELS FOR DAVALLIA (RABBIT'S FOOT FERN) 40

VENTILATION FOR DAVALLIA (RABBIT'S FOOT FERN): MAINTAINING A SUITABLE ENVIRONMENT FOR PLANT HEALTH 43

OPEN TERRARIUM MAINTENANCE FOR DAVALLIA (RABBIT'S FOOT FERN): TRIMMING, PRUNING, AND CLEANING 46

TROUBLESHOOTING COMMON ISSUES FOR DAVALLIA (RABBIT'S FOOT FERN) IN OPEN TERRARIUMS 49

SEASONAL CHANGES AND CARE TIPS FOR DAVALLIA (RABBIT'S FOOT FERN) IN OPEN TERRARIUMS 52

INCORPORATING NATURAL ELEMENTS FOR DAVALLIA (RABBIT'S FOOT FERN): ROCKS, PEBBLES, AND SAND 55

MANAGING INVASIVE GROWTH IN TERRARIUM FOR DAVALLIA (RABBIT'S FOOT FERN) 58

FERTILIZING OPEN TERRARIUMS: NOURISHING DAVALLIA (RABBIT'S FOOT FERN) 61

DEALING WITH PESTS AND DISEASES OF DAVALLIA (RABBIT'S FOOT FERN): STRATEGIES FOR KEEPING YOUR OPEN TERRARIUM HEALTHY 64

DAVALLIA (RABBIT'S FOOT FERN) REPOTTING AND PLANT PROPAGATION: MULTIPLYING PLANTS WITHIN THE OPEN TERRARIUM 67

OPTIMIZING HUMIDITY LEVELS OF DAVALLIA (RABBIT'S FOOT FERN) IN YOUR OPEN TERRARIUM 70

LONG-TERM MAINTENANCE FOR DAVALLIA (RABBIT'S FOOT FERN): REPOTTING, REFRESHING, AND REJUVENATING YOUR OPEN TERRARIUM 73

DESIGNING DAVALLIA (RABBIT'S FOOT FERN) IN YOUR OPEN TERRARIUM: CONSIDERING AESTHETICS AND ARRANGEMENT 76

ENHANCING YOUR TERRARIUM WITH DECORATIVE ELEMENTS FOR DAVALLIA (RABBIT'S FOOT FERN): ADDING VISUAL INTEREST AND CREATIVITY 79

DESIGNING MINIATURE GARDENS FOR DAVALLIA (RABBIT'S FOOT FERN): CONSTRUCTING MINIATURE LANDSCAPES IN YOUR TERRARIUM 82

USING DRIFTWOOD AND BRANCHES FOR DAVALLIA (RABBIT'S FOOT FERN): CREATING NATURAL HABITATS WITHIN THE TERRARIUM 85

CONCLUSION: DAVALLIA (RABBIT'S FOOT FERN) IN TERRARIUM 88

INTRODUCTION TO OPEN TERRARIUM FOR DAVALLIA (RABBIT'S FOOT FERN)

Open terrariums provide an ideal environment for nurturing delicate plants like the Davallia, commonly known as the Rabbit's Foot Fern. This type of fern is particularly well-suited for open terrarium setups due to its unique growth habits and requirements.

UNDERSTANDING THE CONCEPT

An open terrarium is a glass or transparent container that houses plants in an environment designed to mimic a miniature ecosystem. Unlike closed terrariums, which have a sealed environment, open terrariums allow for better airflow and moisture regulation. This is crucial for plants like the Davallia fern, which require some humidity but can't tolerate excessive moisture.

BENEFITS OF AN OPEN TERRARIUM FOR DAVALLIA

Creating an open terrarium for your Davallia fern offers several benefits:

- **Optimal Air Circulation:** The open design ensures proper airflow, preventing the growth of mold and mildew that can be detrimental to the fern's health.
- **Moisture Control:** The fern benefits from controlled humidity levels without the risk of root rot that can occur in closed terrariums.
- **Easy Maintenance:** Open terrariums are simpler to maintain as you don't have to worry about constant humidity monitoring and ventilation adjustment.
- **Aesthetic Appeal:** The transparent container showcases the beauty of the Davallia fern, allowing you to enjoy its intricate foliage.

Overall, an open terrarium provides a visually appealing and nurturing environment for your Davallia (Rabbit's Foot Fern), promoting healthy growth and minimizing the risk of common terrarium issues.

BEAUTY OF OPEN TERRARIUM: A WINDOW INTO MINIATURE LANDSCAPES

Open terrariums offer a captivating way to create and observe miniature landscapes, bringing the beauty of nature into your living space. These living works of art allow you to appreciate the intricacies of plant life up close and provide a unique perspective on the world of botany.

UNVEILING MINIATURE WORLDS

When you peer into an open terrarium, you're met with a mesmerizing glimpse of a small-scale ecosystem. The carefully selected plants, decorative elements like pebbles and figurines, and the interplay of colors and textures form a breathtaking tableau. Each open terrarium becomes a self-contained universe, inviting you to explore its details.

CREATING BREATHTAKING COMPOSITIONS

Open terrariums serve as your canvas to craft stunning compositions. You can experiment with various plant species, arranging them in ways that mimic natural landscapes or allow for imaginative designs. From lush, fern-filled forests to arid desert scenes, your open terrarium can reflect any environment you envision.

ENGAGING THE SENSES

An open terrarium doesn't just engage your visual senses—it stimulates your sense of touch, too. As you tend to your mini landscape, you'll feel the textures of different plants and substrates. The Rabbit's Foot Fern (Davallia) may offer its soft, furry rhizomes to touch, creating a tactile experience that connects you with nature on an intimate level.

BRINGING NATURE INDOORS

Modern living often separates us from the outdoors, but open terrariums bridge that gap. They allow you to bring a piece of nature indoors, creating a serene and refreshing atmosphere. The miniature landscapes provide a sanctuary of tranquility, inviting you to escape from the hustle and bustle of daily life.

A SOURCE OF INSPIRATION

Open terrariums can be a source of inspiration and creativity. They encourage you to learn about different plant species, ecosystems, and gardening techniques. As you care for your miniature landscape, you'll develop a deeper appreciation for the delicate balance of nature.

In conclusion, open terrariums are not just decorative elements; they are windows into enchanting miniature landscapes that offer beauty, wonder, and a sense of connection with the natural world.

CHOOSING THE RIGHT CONTAINER FOR DAVALLIA (RABBIT'S FOOT FERN)

When creating an open terrarium for your Davallia fern, selecting the right container is essential to provide an optimal environment for its growth. The container you choose will impact factors like humidity, air circulation, and aesthetics, all of which contribute to the overall health and beauty of your mini ecosystem.

CONSIDERATIONS FOR CONTAINER SELECTION

Here are some key considerations to keep in mind when choosing the right container for your Davallia fern:

TYPE OF CONTAINER

Opt for a glass or transparent container to allow ample light to reach the fern while showcasing its intricate foliage. A container with an open top ensures proper air circulation, preventing excessive humidity buildup that could harm the fern.

SIZE AND SHAPE

Choose a container with enough space for your Davallia fern to grow comfortably. The size should accommodate the fern's root system and allow for some expansion. A wider base and slightly taller height can provide a sense of depth and allow for creative landscaping within the terrarium.

DRAINAGE

While open terrariums don't require the same level of drainage as closed ones, it's still essential to avoid waterlogged soil. Ensure that your chosen container has small drainage holes or a layer of gravel at the bottom to prevent water from pooling around the roots of the fern.

AESTHETICS AND DESIGN

Consider the aesthetic appeal of the container. A container that complements your home decor can enhance the visual impact of your open terrarium. Additionally, the container's design can influence the arrangement of plants, decorative elements, and landscaping within the terrarium.

MAINTAINING THE IDEAL ENVIRONMENT

By selecting the right container, you lay the foundation for a successful open terrarium housing your Davallia fern. The container's features should work in harmony with the fern's requirements for light, air, and moisture, promoting a healthy and thriving mini ecosystem.

In conclusion, choosing the right container for your Davallia (Rabbit's Foot Fern) open terrarium is a crucial step that contributes to the overall beauty and well-being of your miniature landscape.

ESSENTIAL TOOLS AND MATERIALS FOR DAVALLIA (RABBIT'S FOOT FERN) TERRARIUM

Creating a successful open terrarium for your Davallia fern requires the right tools and materials to ensure proper growth and maintenance. Equipping yourself with the necessary supplies will set the stage for a thriving mini ecosystem that showcases the beauty of your fern.

MUST-HAVE TOOLS

Here are some essential tools you'll need for your Davallia fern terrarium:

1. GLASS CONTAINER

Choose a transparent container that allows light in and provides a clear view of your fern. A glass container is the preferred option, as it's durable and aesthetically pleasing.

2. POTTING MIX

Select a well-draining potting mix suitable for ferns. Avoid mixes that retain too much moisture, as the

Davallia fern prefers slightly damp soil without becoming waterlogged.

3. PEBBLES OR GRAVEL

These materials create a drainage layer at the bottom of the container to prevent water accumulation around the roots. This is especially important for maintaining optimal moisture levels.

4. ACTIVATED CHARCOAL

Activated charcoal helps to filter and purify the air within the terrarium, preventing odors and microbial growth. A thin layer at the bottom of the container is sufficient.

ADDITIONAL MATERIALS

In addition to the essential tools, consider the following materials:

1. DECORATIVE ELEMENTS

Add personality to your terrarium with decorative stones, mini figurines, or natural elements like driftwood. These elements can complement the Davallia fern's aesthetic and create a visually appealing arrangement.

2. SPRAY BOTTLE

For misting and maintaining humidity levels, a spray bottle is handy. The Davallia fern benefits from occasional misting, especially in drier environments.

3. WATERING CAN OR SYRINGE

To water your fern, choose a tool that allows precise and controlled watering. A small watering can or a syringe can be useful for avoiding overwatering.

SETTING THE STAGE FOR SUCCESS

Gathering the right tools and materials is the first step towards creating a thriving Davallia (Rabbit's Foot Fern) terrarium. With these supplies, you'll be well-equipped to provide the ideal environment for your fern's growth, ensuring a stunning and healthy mini ecosystem.

SOIL AND SUBSTRATE FOR DAVALLIA (RABBIT'S FOOT FERN) TERRARIUM

The choice of soil and substrate for your Davallia fern terrarium is crucial for its overall health and growth. Creating a well-draining and nutrient-rich medium is essential to provide the fern with the ideal conditions for root development and sustained vitality.

CREATING A WELL-DRAINING MEDIUM

The Davallia fern prefers a soil mix that is well-draining and slightly acidic. Here's how to achieve that:

1. POTTING MIX

Choose a potting mix specifically formulated for ferns or orchids. These mixes typically contain ingredients like peat moss, perlite, and pine bark, ensuring good drainage while retaining enough moisture for the fern's roots.

2. PERLITE OR VERMICULITE

Adding perlite or vermiculite to the mix can further enhance drainage and aeration. These lightweight materials prevent the soil from becoming compacted and help maintain proper airflow.

ENSURING NUTRIENT-RICH SOIL

A nutrient-rich substrate is essential to support the Davallia fern's growth and overall health:

1. ORGANIC MATTER

Incorporate well-rotted organic matter, such as compost or leaf mold, into the potting mix. This provides essential nutrients and promotes healthy root development.

2. SLOW-RELEASE FERTILIZER

Consider adding a slow-release fertilizer formulated for ferns. This ensures a steady supply of nutrients over time, preventing over-fertilization and potential damage to the fern.

LAYERING THE SUBSTRATE

Properly layering the substrate in your terrarium is essential:

1. DRAINAGE LAYER

Begin with a layer of pebbles or gravel at the bottom of the container to facilitate drainage and prevent water accumulation around the roots.

2. CHARCOAL

Place a thin layer of activated charcoal above the drainage layer. This helps keep the terrarium environment fresh and odor-free by absorbing impurities.

3. POTTING MIX

Add the prepared potting mix, ensuring that it's well-compacted but not too tightly packed. Leave enough space for planting the fern and other decorative elements.

CREATING AN IDEAL HABITAT

The soil and substrate you choose play a critical role in creating an ideal habitat for your Davallia (Rabbit's Foot Fern) terrarium. By providing the right balance of drainage and nutrients, you'll set the stage for a lush and thriving mini ecosystem.

LIGHT REQUIREMENTS FOR DAVALLIA (RABBIT'S FOOT FERN)

Providing the right amount and type of light is crucial for the health and well-being of your Davallia fern in an open terrarium. Understanding the fern's light preferences will help you create an environment that promotes its growth and showcases its graceful foliage.

DETERMINING THE IDEAL LIGHT CONDITIONS

The Davallia fern thrives in low to moderate indirect light:

1. INDIRECT LIGHT

Place your open terrarium in a location where it receives indirect sunlight. Avoid exposing the fern to direct sunlight, as it can scorch the delicate fronds and cause damage.

2. BRIGHT BUT FILTERED LIGHT

An ideal spot is near a window with sheer curtains or in a well-lit room that doesn't receive direct sunbeams. The fern will benefit from the gentle, filtered light that promotes photosynthesis without causing stress.

MONITORING LIGHT INTENSITY

Regularly monitor the light intensity to ensure the Davallia fern's well-being:

1. ADJUST PLACEMENT

If you notice the fern's fronds becoming pale or yellowish, it may indicate insufficient light. Gradually move the terrarium to a slightly brighter location, but avoid sudden exposure to intense sunlight.

2. LEAF ORIENTATION

Observe the orientation of the fronds. The Davallia fern's fronds naturally arch towards the light source. Rotate the terrarium periodically to ensure even growth and prevent lopsided foliage.

CREATING THE PERFECT LIGHTING BALANCE

Striking the right balance between light and shade is essential for your Davallia (Rabbit's Foot Fern) open terrarium. By providing the fern with the *appropriate amount of indirect light, you'll ensure its graceful growth and maintain the terrarium's enchanting appearance.*

TEMPERATURE CONSIDERATIONS FOR DAVALLIA (RABBIT'S FOOT FERN)

Creating the right temperature conditions is vital for the well-being of your Davallia fern within an open terrarium. Understanding the fern's temperature preferences will help you provide a comfortable environment that promotes its growth and vitality.

UNDERSTANDING TEMPERATURE RANGE

The Davallia fern prefers a temperature range that mimics its natural habitat:

1. MODERATE TEMPERATURES

Maintain the terrarium in an area with moderate room temperatures. Ideal temperatures generally fall between 60°F (15°C) and 75°F (24°C).

2. AVOID EXTREMES

Avoid exposing the fern to drastic temperature fluctuations or extremes. Keep the terrarium away from drafts, direct heat sources, and air conditioning vents.

MONITORING AND ADJUSTING

Consistently monitor the temperature and make necessary adjustments:

1. THERMOMETER

Place a thermometer near the terrarium to track temperature variations. This will help you ensure that the fern is within its preferred temperature range.

2. SEASONAL CHANGES

During colder months, protect the fern from cold drafts and consider moving it slightly closer to a heat source, as long as the temperature remains within the suitable range.

CREATING AN OPTIMAL HABITAT

By understanding and catering to the temperature needs of your Davallia (Rabbit's Foot Fern), you're creating an optimal habitat for its growth and well-being. Providing consistent and comfortable temperatures will contribute to the fern's lush and vibrant appearance.

STEP-BY-STEP GUIDE TO BUILDING YOUR OPEN TERRARIUM FOR DAVALLIA (RABBIT'S FOOT FERN)

Creating a beautiful and thriving open terrarium for your Davallia fern is a rewarding endeavor. Follow this step-by-step guide to build a captivating mini ecosystem that showcases the charm of your fern.

STEP 1: GATHER YOUR SUPPLIES

Collect all the necessary tools and materials:

- Glass container
- Potting mix suitable for ferns
- Pebbles or gravel
- Activated charcoal
- Decorative elements (stones, figurines, etc.)
- Spray bottle
- Watering can or syringe

STEP 2: PREPARE THE CONTAINER

Set up the foundation of your terrarium:

1. Add a layer of pebbles or gravel for drainage.
2. Place a thin layer of activated charcoal to keep the environment fresh.
3. Add the potting mix, leaving space for planting and arranging.

STEP 3: PLANTING YOUR DAVALLIA FERN

Carefully plant your Davallia fern:

1. Gently remove the fern from its nursery pot and shake off excess soil.
2. Make a hole in the potting mix and place the fern's root system into it.
3. Fill around the roots with additional potting mix, ensuring the fern is stable.

STEP 4: ADDING DECORATIVE ELEMENTS

Enhance the visual appeal of your terrarium:

1. Arrange decorative elements like stones, figurines, or driftwood to create a pleasing composition.
2. Use a spray bottle to mist the fern and decorative elements with water.

STEP 5: PLACEMENT AND CARE

Find the perfect spot for your terrarium and provide ongoing care:

1. Place the terrarium in a location with indirect sunlight and suitable room temperature.
2. Monitor the light, humidity, and moisture levels, adjusting as needed.
3. Mist the fern and terrarium occasionally to maintain humidity.

4. Water the fern when the top inch of the soil feels slightly dry, avoiding overwatering.
5. Rotate the terrarium periodically for even growth.

STEP 6: ENJOY AND MAINTAIN

Admire your creation and provide ongoing care:

- Observe the fern's growth and make adjustments to lighting and care as needed.
- Prune any dead or yellowing fronds to maintain the fern's appearance.
- Continue to mist, water, and maintain the terrarium to ensure the fern's well-being.

With dedication and care, your Davallia (Rabbit's Foot Fern) open terrarium will become a captivating centerpiece, bringing a touch of nature's beauty into your living space.

PREPARING THE CONTAINER FOR DAVALLIA (RABBIT'S FOOT FERN) TERRARIUM

Before you begin planting your Davallia fern, proper preparation of the container is essential to ensure a healthy and visually appealing mini ecosystem. Follow these steps to clean and set up the container for your terrarium.

STEP 1: SELECTING THE CONTAINER

Choose an appropriate container for your open terrarium:

- Select a glass or transparent container to allow light and visibility.
- Ensure the container is clean and free from any residues or dirt.
- Consider the size and shape, allowing enough space for the fern's growth and decorative elements.

STEP 2: CLEANING THE CONTAINER

Thoroughly clean the container before planting:

1. Wash the container with mild soap and water, rinsing it thoroughly to remove any soap residues.

2. Use a mixture of water and vinegar to remove mineral deposits or hard water stains.
3. Allow the container to dry completely to prevent moisture buildup in the terrarium.

STEP 3: ADDING LAYERS

Create a suitable foundation for your terrarium:

1. Add a layer of pebbles or gravel at the bottom of the container for drainage.
2. Place a thin layer of activated charcoal over the drainage layer to absorb impurities.
3. Top it off with a layer of potting mix, leaving space for planting.

STEP 4: POSITIONING THE CONTAINER

Find the perfect spot for your prepared container:

- Place the container in a location with the right light conditions (indirect sunlight) and suitable room temperature.
- Avoid exposing the container to direct heat sources or cold drafts.

STEP 5: READY FOR PLANTING

With your container cleaned, layered, and positioned appropriately, it's now ready for planting your

Davallia (Rabbit's Foot Fern) and creating a captivating open terrarium that will enhance your living space.

PREPARING THE BASE LAYER OF YOUR OPEN TERRARIUM FOR DAVALLIA (RABBIT'S FOOT FERN)

The base layer of your open terrarium serves as the foundation for creating a well-draining and visually appealing environment for your Davallia fern. Follow these steps to establish the base layer in your terrarium.

STEP 1: SELECTING THE MATERIALS

Choose the right materials for the base layer:

- Opt for small pebbles or gravel that are clean and free from dust or contaminants.
- Ensure the size of the pebbles allows adequate water drainage without clogging.

STEP 2: CREATING THE DRAINAGE LAYER

Establish the drainage layer at the bottom of the terrarium:

1. Add a layer of small pebbles or gravel about 1 to 2 inches deep at the base of the container.
2. Distribute the layer evenly to ensure proper water drainage throughout the terrarium.

3. The drainage layer prevents water from accumulating around the roots and causing root rot.

STEP 3: BENEFITS OF THE BASE LAYER

The base layer provides multiple benefits for your Davallia fern terrarium:

- **Prevents Waterlogging:** The drainage layer prevents excess water from pooling around the roots.
- **Facilitates Air Circulation:** Adequate drainage enhances airflow through the substrate, preventing soil compaction.
- **Reduces Risk of Root Rot:** Proper drainage minimizes the risk of root diseases caused by overly wet conditions.

STEP 4: MOVING FORWARD

With the base layer in place, you've created a solid foundation for your open terrarium. The next steps will involve adding activated charcoal and the potting mix, allowing you to build a suitable habitat for your Davallia (Rabbit's Foot Fern) that combines functionality and aesthetics.

ADDING THE GROWING MEDIUM AND OPTIMIZING SOIL CONDITIONS FOR DAVALLIA (RABBIT'S FOOT FERN)

Creating the right soil conditions is essential to ensure the health and vitality of your Davallia fern within an open terrarium. Follow these steps to add the growing medium and optimize soil conditions for your fern's growth.

STEP 1: CHOOSING THE POTTING MIX

Select a suitable potting mix for your Davallia fern:

- Choose a potting mix formulated for ferns or orchids, which typically provides good drainage.
- The mix should be well-aerated and able to hold moisture without becoming waterlogged.

STEP 2: ADDING THE POTTING MIX

Introduce the potting mix to your terrarium:

1. Add the potting mix on top of the drainage layer, leaving space for planting and decorative elements.
2. Ensure an even distribution of the mix to promote uniform moisture throughout the terrarium.

3. The depth of the potting mix should be suitable for accommodating the fern's root system.

STEP 3: CREATING OPTIMAL SOIL CONDITIONS

Optimize the soil conditions to support your Davallia fern's growth:

- Moisture: The potting mix should be slightly damp but not waterlogged. Maintain consistent moisture levels to prevent drying out or oversaturation.
- Drainage: The well-draining mix and drainage layer help prevent excess water accumulation, reducing the risk of root rot.
- Nutrition: The potting mix should contain organic matter and nutrients to support the fern's growth. Consider adding slow-release fertilizer designed for ferns.
- pH Levels: Aim for a slightly acidic to neutral pH range (around 5.5 to 7) for optimal nutrient availability.

STEP 4: MAINTAINING THE SOIL

Regularly monitor and maintain the soil conditions:

- Check the moisture level by feeling the top inch of the soil. Water when it's slightly dry.
- Avoid allowing the potting mix to become bone-dry or overly soggy.

- Monitor plant health and adjust watering and care as needed.

STEP 5: NURTURING HEALTHY GROWTH

With the growing medium prepared and soil conditions optimized, you're setting the stage for healthy and vibrant growth of your Davallia (Rabbit's Foot Fern) within the open terrarium.

ARRANGING DAVALLIA (RABBIT'S FOOT FERN) IN YOUR OPEN TERRARIUM

The arrangement of your Davallia fern within the open terrarium is both an art and a science. Careful positioning and consideration of aesthetics will help you create an appealing and harmonious mini landscape that showcases the beauty of your fern.

STEP 1: SELECTING THE FOCUS POINT

Choose a focal point for your arrangement:

- Select the main location where you want the Davallia fern to be the center of attention.
- This could be the center, a corner, or a visually appealing spot in your terrarium.

STEP 2: POSITIONING THE FERN

Place the Davallia fern in the terrarium:

1. Position the fern's root system gently into the potting mix at the chosen focal point.
2. Arrange the fronds to face outward and slightly upward, showcasing their graceful growth habit.
3. Consider the fern's mature size when arranging to ensure it has space to grow.

STEP 3: ADDING DECORATIVE ELEMENTS

Enhance the arrangement with decorative elements:

1. Place decorative stones, figurines, or driftwood around the fern to complement its beauty.
2. Create a balanced and visually appealing composition by varying the height and texture of the elements.
3. Ensure the decorative elements don't overcrowd or overshadow the fern.

STEP 4: BALANCING AND VISUAL FLOW

Ensure a harmonious visual flow in the arrangement:

- Step back and observe the terrarium from different angles to assess the balance of the arrangement.
- Avoid placing elements in a way that directs attention away from the focal point.
- Experiment with different positions until you achieve a satisfying composition.

STEP 5: REFLECTING YOUR STYLE

Let your personal style shine through:

- Arrange elements in a way that resonates with your aesthetic preferences.

- Consider the colors, textures, and themes that match your home decor.
- Remember that your open terrarium is an expression of your creativity.

STEP 6: ADMIRE AND ADJUST

By thoughtfully arranging your Davallia (Rabbit's Foot Fern) and decorative elements, you've crafted a captivating visual masterpiece in your open terrarium. Regularly observe and make minor adjustments to maintain the arrangement's beauty as your fern thrives.

PROPER DRAINAGE TECHNIQUES FOR DAVALLIA (RABBIT'S FOOT FERN) IN OPEN TERRARIUMS

Ensuring adequate drainage is essential for maintaining a healthy and thriving Davallia fern within an open terrarium. Follow these drainage techniques to prevent water accumulation and promote optimal growth for your fern.

STEP 1: LAYERING THE DRAINAGE SYSTEM

Establish a layered drainage system in your terrarium:

1. Add a layer of small pebbles or gravel at the bottom of the container. This layer allows excess water to collect and drain away from the soil.
2. Ensure the drainage layer is about 1 to 2 inches deep for effective water movement.

STEP 2: USING ACTIVATED CHARCOAL

Incorporate activated charcoal into the drainage system:

1. Place a thin layer of activated charcoal over the pebble layer. Activated charcoal helps absorb

impurities and prevents odor buildup in the terrarium.
2. This layer enhances the overall freshness of the terrarium environment.

STEP 3: SELECTING A WELL-DRAINING POTTING MIX

Choose the right potting mix to ensure proper drainage:

- Select a potting mix formulated for ferns or orchids, which typically have good drainage properties.
- Avoid heavy or compacted soils that can hinder water movement.

STEP 4: MONITORING WATERING HABITS

Regularly monitor and adjust your watering practices:

- Water the fern only when the top inch of the soil feels slightly dry.
- Avoid overwatering, as it can lead to waterlogged conditions and root rot.
- Watering should provide enough moisture for the fern without causing excess runoff.

STEP 5: PROPER TERRARIUM PLACEMENT

Choose the right location for your open terrarium:

- Place the terrarium in a spot with indirect sunlight and suitable room temperature.
- Avoid exposing the terrarium to extreme temperatures or drafts, which can affect moisture levels and drainage.

STEP 6: OBSERVING AND ADJUSTING

By implementing these drainage techniques, you're creating a balanced and supportive environment for your Davallia (Rabbit's Foot Fern) in the open terrarium. Regularly observe the moisture levels and adjust your care routine as needed to maintain optimal drainage and prevent water-related issues.

WATERING TECHNIQUES AND MAINTAINING PROPER MOISTURE LEVELS FOR DAVALLIA (RABBIT'S FOOT FERN)

Proper watering is crucial for the health and vitality of your Davallia fern within an open terrarium. Follow these watering techniques to maintain appropriate moisture levels and provide optimal care for your fern.

STEP 1: MONITORING SOIL MOISTURE

Regularly check the soil moisture in the terrarium:

- Use your finger to feel the top inch of the soil.
- Water the fern when the soil feels slightly dry to the touch.
- Avoid letting the soil become bone-dry or overly saturated.

STEP 2: WATERING METHOD

Choose an appropriate watering method for your terrarium:

- Use a syringe, small watering can, or spray bottle to water the fern gently.

- Direct the water towards the base of the fern to avoid wetting the fronds excessively.
- Ensure water doesn't accumulate in the terrarium and promote proper drainage.

STEP 3: FREQUENCY OF WATERING

Establish a consistent watering routine:

- Water the Davallia fern when the top inch of the soil feels slightly dry.
- Frequency may vary based on environmental factors like temperature and humidity.
- Err on the side of slightly underwatering rather than overwatering.

STEP 4: PREVENTING OVERWATERING

Avoid overwatering to prevent root issues:

- Ensure the terrarium has proper drainage to prevent water from accumulating.
- Don't allow the fern's roots to sit in standing water.
- Excess moisture can lead to root rot and other fungal problems.

STEP 5: ADJUSTING WATERING HABITS

Observe your fern's response to watering:

- If the fronds become pale or yellow, it may indicate overwatering.

- If the fronds wilt or the soil feels extremely dry, adjust your watering routine.
- Adapt your watering based on your fern's specific needs and the conditions in your home.

STEP 6: CONSISTENCY AND CARE

By following these watering techniques and maintaining proper moisture levels, you're providing attentive care for your Davallia (Rabbit's Foot Fern) in the open terrarium. Consistent and balanced watering will contribute to the fern's lush and vibrant growth.

VENTILATION FOR DAVALLIA (RABBIT'S FOOT FERN): MAINTAINING A SUITABLE ENVIRONMENT FOR PLANT HEALTH

Proper ventilation is crucial for creating a healthy and thriving environment for your Davallia fern within an open terrarium. Follow these guidelines to ensure adequate airflow and maintain optimal conditions for your fern's growth.

STEP 1: IMPORTANCE OF VENTILATION

Understand the significance of ventilation in an open terrarium:

- Ventilation promotes air exchange, preventing the buildup of stagnant air and excess moisture.
- It helps regulate temperature, humidity, and prevents fungal issues that thrive in humid environments.
- Proper airflow supports photosynthesis and overall plant health.

STEP 2: CHOOSING THE RIGHT LOCATION

Select an appropriate spot for your terrarium:

- Place the terrarium in an area with indirect sunlight and suitable room temperature.
- Avoid locations with poor air circulation, such as closed cabinets or corners.

STEP 3: REGULAR TERRARIUM ROTATION

Rotate the terrarium periodically:

- Gently turn the terrarium to different angles to expose all sides to fresh air and light.
- This prevents one side from receiving excessive moisture or reduced airflow.

STEP 4: PARTIAL TERRARIUM OPENING

Occasionally partially open the terrarium:

- Depending on the design, partially lift the lid or remove a cover to allow fresh air to enter.
- Do this for a short period to prevent rapid changes in temperature or humidity.

STEP 5: MONITORING AND ADJUSTING

Regularly assess the terrarium's conditions:

- Observe the fern's health and check for signs of excessive moisture or poor ventilation.
- Adjust the terrarium's position and ventilation practices based on your observations.

STEP 6: STRIKING A BALANCE

By maintaining proper ventilation, you're striking a balance between humidity and airflow that's ideal for your Davallia (Rabbit's Foot Fern). A well-ventilated terrarium provides the fern with the best possible environment for robust growth and a stunning appearance.

OPEN TERRARIUM MAINTENANCE FOR DAVALLIA (RABBIT'S FOOT FERN): TRIMMING, PRUNING, AND CLEANING

Maintaining your open terrarium is essential for ensuring the health and beauty of your Davallia fern. Follow these maintenance tasks of trimming, pruning, and cleaning to promote your fern's well-being and keep your terrarium looking stunning.

STEP 1: REGULAR TRIMMING

Trim the fern's fronds as needed:

- Use clean, sharp scissors or pruning shears to trim any yellowing or browned fronds.
- Remove dead or damaged foliage to encourage new growth and maintain the fern's appearance.
- Prune with care to avoid injuring healthy parts of the plant.

STEP 2: PRUNING FOR SPACE

Prune to manage the fern's size and shape:

- If the fern becomes too large for the terrarium, trim back excessive growth to maintain a balanced arrangement.

- Prune selectively to shape the fern and prevent it from overcrowding other plants or decorative elements.

STEP 3: CLEANING THE TERRARIUM

Keep the terrarium clean for optimal visibility and plant health:

- Remove any fallen leaves, debris, or dust from the surface of the soil.
- Gently wipe the inside of the terrarium's glass walls to maintain clarity and allow light to penetrate.
- Regular cleaning prevents the buildup of mold, algae, or pests.

STEP 4: MONITORING FOR PESTS

Be vigilant for signs of pests:

- Check the fern and the terrarium for any pests such as mites, aphids, or mealybugs.
- If pests are detected, isolate the affected plant and take appropriate measures to control the infestation.

STEP 5: MAINTENANCE SCHEDULE

Establish a regular maintenance routine:

- Set a schedule for trimming, pruning, and cleaning based on the fern's growth rate and terrarium conditions.
- Consistent care ensures the fern's health and keeps your open terrarium looking its best.

STEP 6: ENRICHING YOUR TERRARIUM EXPERIENCE

By performing these maintenance tasks, you're enriching your experience with the Davallia (Rabbit's Foot Fern) in the open terrarium. Regular care and attention will result in a thriving fern and a captivating mini ecosystem that brings joy and beauty to your space.

TROUBLESHOOTING COMMON ISSUES FOR DAVALLIA (RABBIT'S FOOT FERN) IN OPEN TERRARIUMS

Even with proper care, challenges can arise when cultivating your Davallia fern in an open terrarium. Learn how to identify and address common issues to ensure your fern's health and the longevity of your terrarium ecosystem.

STEP 1: YELLOWING OR BROWNING FRONDS

Address fronds that show signs of discoloration:

- Yellowing fronds may indicate overwatering or improper drainage.
- Browning frond tips can result from underwatering, low humidity, or direct sunlight.
- Adjust watering practices and humidity levels to restore healthy frond color.

STEP 2: WILTING OR DROOPING FRONDS

Revive wilting or drooping fronds:

- Wilting may occur due to underwatering or inadequate moisture levels.

- Drooping can result from poor drainage, overwatering, or excessive humidity.
- Assess the soil moisture and adjust watering as needed to revive frond turgidity.

STEP 3: BROWN OR BLACK SPOTS ON FRONDS

Address brown or black spots on fronds:

- Spots may be caused by fungal or bacterial issues due to excess moisture.
- Ensure proper ventilation, avoid overcrowding, and maintain balanced moisture.
- Remove affected fronds and improve airflow to prevent further spread.

STEP 4: PEST INFESTATIONS

Combat pest infestations effectively:

- Check the fern regularly for signs of pests like mites, aphids, or mealybugs.
- Isolate affected plants, remove pests manually, or use natural pest control methods.
- Maintain good hygiene and airflow to discourage pests from taking hold.

STEP 5: ADJUSTING LIGHT AND TEMPERATURE

Address issues related to light and temperature:

- Yellowing fronds with weak growth may result from insufficient light.
- Direct sunlight can scorch fronds and cause dryness.
- Adjust the terrarium's placement to provide appropriate light and maintain a consistent temperature range.

STEP 6: CONSISTENT OBSERVATION AND ADAPTATION

By troubleshooting these common issues, you're ensuring a healthy environment for your Davallia (Rabbit's Foot Fern) within the open terrarium. Consistently observe your fern and adapt your care routine based on its response, fostering a thriving mini ecosystem that brings beauty to your space.

SEASONAL CHANGES AND CARE TIPS FOR DAVALLIA (RABBIT'S FOOT FERN) IN OPEN TERRARIUMS

Adapting your care routine to the changing seasons is essential for the well-being of your Davallia fern in an open terrarium. Explore these seasonal care tips to ensure your fern thrives year-round and continues to beautify your space.

STEP 1: SPRING CARE

Adjust care as spring arrives:

- As the days lengthen, your fern may experience increased growth.
- Inspect the terrarium for signs of overgrowth or overcrowding, and consider pruning if necessary.
- Monitor soil moisture and adapt watering frequency based on the fern's response to changing temperatures.

STEP 2: SUMMER CARE

Provide extra attention during summer:

- Increased sunlight and temperatures may lead to faster evaporation of moisture.
- Monitor soil moisture levels closely and water more frequently if necessary.

- Consider moving the terrarium to a spot with filtered sunlight to prevent direct exposure.

STEP 3: FALL CARE

Prepare for fall's changing conditions:

- As temperatures cool, the fern's growth may slow down.
- Reduce watering frequency and avoid waterlogging the soil.
- Ensure the terrarium maintains suitable humidity levels to support the fern's health.

STEP 4: WINTER CARE

Adjust care for winter's conditions:

- Cooler temperatures and lower light levels may result in slower growth.
- Water the fern sparingly and allow the top inch of the soil to dry out between waterings.
- Ensure the terrarium is placed in a stable environment with consistent temperatures.

STEP 5: ONGOING OBSERVATION

Continuously monitor your fern's needs:

- Observe how the Davallia fern responds to seasonal changes and adjust care accordingly.
- Regularly assess the terrarium's moisture, light exposure, and overall health.

- Adapting your care routine ensures the fern's well-being throughout the year.

STEP 6: A YEAR-ROUND BEAUTY

By tailoring your care to the changing seasons, you're embracing the natural rhythm of your Davallia (Rabbit's Foot Fern) in the open terrarium. Each season presents unique opportunities to nurture and enjoy the fern's beauty, resulting in a stunning display that delights you year-round.

INCORPORATING NATURAL ELEMENTS FOR DAVALLIA (RABBIT'S FOOT FERN): ROCKS, PEBBLES, AND SAND

Enhancing your open terrarium with natural elements like rocks, pebbles, and sand adds visual interest and complements the beauty of your Davallia fern. Learn how to incorporate these elements creatively to create a harmonious and captivating mini landscape.

STEP 1: SELECTION OF NATURAL ELEMENTS

Choose rocks, pebbles, and sand that suit your terrarium's theme:

- Opt for materials that harmonize with the fern's color and growth habit.
- Consider the size and texture of the elements to create a balanced arrangement.
- Ensure the materials are clean and free of contaminants.

STEP 2: BASE LAYER OF ROCKS OR PEBBLES

Create a base layer of rocks or pebbles:

- Place a 1 to 2-inch layer of small rocks or pebbles at the bottom of the terrarium for drainage.
- This layer promotes proper water movement and prevents water accumulation.

STEP 3: SAND FOR AESTHETIC APPEAL

Incorporate sand for visual appeal:

- Add a thin layer of sand above the rocks or pebbles for texture and aesthetics.
- Choose a sand color that complements the fern and the overall terrarium design.
- Ensure the sand layer is not too thick, as it may affect drainage.

STEP 4: CREATIVE ARRANGEMENT

Arrange natural elements creatively around the fern:

- Position larger rocks or decorative stones strategically to create focal points.
- Distribute smaller pebbles and sand to add texture and depth to the arrangement.
- Avoid overcrowding and maintain a balanced composition.

STEP 5: REFLECTING NATURAL LANDSCAPES

Imitate natural landscapes with your arrangements:

- Consider the fern's origin and habitat when arranging natural elements.
- Create a miniature landscape that evokes a forest floor or a rocky woodland environment.
- Let your creativity and inspiration guide your arrangement.

STEP 6: AESTHETIC AND BOTANIC FUSION

By incorporating rocks, pebbles, and sand, you're fusing aesthetic beauty with the natural charm of the Davallia (Rabbit's Foot Fern) in the open terrarium. Your thoughtful arrangement elevates the terrarium into a captivating visual masterpiece that celebrates the wonders of nature.

MANAGING INVASIVE GROWTH IN TERRARIUM FOR DAVALLIA (RABBIT'S FOOT FERN)

Preventing and managing invasive growth in your terrarium is crucial to maintaining the health and balance of your Davallia fern. Learn effective strategies to keep the fern's growth under control and ensure a thriving and harmonious terrarium environment.

STEP 1: REGULAR OBSERVATION

Regularly monitor your terrarium's growth:

- Keep an eye on the Davallia fern's growth patterns and spread.
- Identify any fronds or shoots that are growing rapidly and dominating the space.
- Early detection helps prevent invasive growth from taking over the terrarium.

STEP 2: PRUNING AND TRIMMING

Prune and trim excessively invasive growth:

- Use clean and sharp scissors or pruning shears to remove overgrown fronds or shoots.

- Frequent pruning prevents the fern from becoming overcrowded and allows space for other plants and decorative elements.
- Prune selectively to maintain the fern's shape and appearance.

STEP 3: PROPAGATION CONTROL

Control propagation to prevent overgrowth:

- If the fern is producing too many offshoots, consider limiting the propagation by removing some of them.
- Propagate the fern only when necessary to maintain a manageable size within the terrarium.

STEP 4: PROPER SPACING

Space out plants appropriately:

- When arranging the terrarium, ensure plants have enough space to grow without overcrowding each other.
- Avoid placing plants too close, which can lead to competition for light and nutrients.

STEP 5: TERRARIUM REORGANIZATION

Reorganize the terrarium periodically:

- Gently move and rearrange plants to create balance and prevent one plant from dominating the space.

- Shift decorative elements and natural elements to accommodate the fern's growth and maintain a harmonious arrangement.

STEP 6: NURTURING HARMONY

By managing invasive growth, you're nurturing harmony within your terrarium while showcasing the beauty of the Davallia (Rabbit's Foot Fern). A well-maintained and balanced terrarium environment ensures that all elements can flourish and contribute to the captivating appeal of your miniature ecosystem.

FERTILIZING OPEN TERRARIUMS: NOURISHING DAVALLIA (RABBIT'S FOOT FERN)

Fertilizing your open terrarium is essential to provide the necessary nutrients for your Davallia fern's growth and vitality. Learn how to properly nourish your fern within the terrarium environment to support its health and enhance its beauty.

STEP 1: UNDERSTANDING FERTILIZER NEEDS

Recognize the nutrient requirements of your fern:

- Davallia ferns are generally low to moderate feeders and don't require heavy fertilization.
- Choose a balanced, water-soluble fertilizer with a low concentration to prevent over-fertilization.
- Look for fertilizers with a balanced N-P-K ratio, which indicates the proportion of nitrogen, phosphorus, and potassium.

STEP 2: FERTILIZING FREQUENCY

Establish a regular fertilizing schedule:

- Fertilize the fern once every 1 to 2 months during the growing season (spring and summer).

- Reduce or cease fertilization during fall and winter when the fern's growth slows down.
- Over-fertilization can lead to salt buildup and damage the fern's roots.

STEP 3: DILUTION AND APPLICATION

Dilute the fertilizer and apply it correctly:

- Follow the manufacturer's instructions for dilution and application rates.
- Generally, dilute the fertilizer to half or one-quarter of the recommended strength for indoor plants.
- Apply the diluted fertilizer to the soil surface, avoiding direct contact with the fern's fronds.

STEP 4: WATERING AFTER FERTILIZATION

Water the terrarium after fertilizing:

- After applying the diluted fertilizer, water the terrarium lightly to ensure even distribution of nutrients in the soil.
- Proper watering helps prevent the accumulation of fertilizer salts on the soil surface.

STEP 5: MONITORING RESPONSE

Observe the fern's response to fertilization:

- If the fern shows signs of over-fertilization, such as burnt or browned tips, reduce the frequency or strength of fertilization.
- If growth is slow or the fern appears pale, consider adjusting the fertilizing schedule or strength.

STEP 6: BALANCED NUTRITION FOR BEAUTY

By fertilizing your open terrarium, you're providing balanced nutrition to enhance the beauty and health of your Davallia (Rabbit's Foot Fern). Thoughtful fertilization ensures that your fern thrives within the terrarium environment, contributing to a captivating and vibrant display.

DEALING WITH PESTS AND DISEASES OF DAVALLIA (RABBIT'S FOOT FERN): STRATEGIES FOR KEEPING YOUR OPEN TERRARIUM HEALTHY

Maintaining a pest-free and disease-resistant environment is essential for the well-being of your Davallia fern in the open terrarium. Learn effective strategies to prevent, identify, and address potential pest and disease issues to ensure the longevity and beauty of your miniature ecosystem.

STEP 1: REGULAR INSPECTION

Conduct routine inspections of your terrarium:

- Frequently examine the fern's foliage, stems, and the terrarium's overall health.
- Look for signs of pests such as mites, aphids, mealybugs, or other insects.
- Identify any unusual discoloration, spots, or wilting that may indicate diseases.

STEP 2: ISOLATION OF AFFECTED PLANTS

Isolate plants showing signs of pests or diseases:

- If you detect a pest or disease issue, promptly remove the affected plant from the terrarium.
- Place the isolated plant in an area away from other plants to prevent the issue from spreading.

STEP 3: NATURAL REMEDIES

Utilize natural remedies for pest control:

- Use neem oil, insecticidal soap, or diluted dish soap as natural sprays to deter pests.
- Introduce beneficial insects like ladybugs that feed on harmful pests.
- Regularly clean the terrarium to minimize the likelihood of pest infestations.

STEP 4: DISEASE MANAGEMENT

Address and manage diseases appropriately:

- Trim and remove affected plant parts to prevent the spread of diseases.
- Avoid overwatering and improve ventilation to reduce the risk of fungal infections.
- If necessary, treat with appropriate fungicides or remedies recommended for specific diseases.

STEP 5: PREVENTIVE MEASURES

Take preventive measures to maintain terrarium health:

- Ensure proper drainage to prevent waterlogged soil, which can attract pests and lead to root rot.
- Maintain optimal humidity levels to discourage both pests and diseases.
- Regularly clean and sanitize the terrarium and its components to prevent buildup of mold and pathogens.

STEP 6: ENSURING LONG-TERM HEALTH

By addressing pests and diseases effectively, you're ensuring the long-term health and vibrancy of your Davallia (Rabbit's Foot Fern) and its open terrarium. Your vigilance and proactive measures contribute to the overall beauty and success of your miniature ecosystem.

DAVALLIA (RABBIT'S FOOT FERN) REPOTTING AND PLANT PROPAGATION: MULTIPLYING PLANTS WITHIN THE OPEN TERRARIUM

Repotting and propagating your Davallia fern within the open terrarium can help you create a lush and thriving mini ecosystem. Learn the techniques for repotting and propagating your fern to expand its presence and enhance the beauty of your terrarium.

STEP 1: ASSESSING THE NEED FOR REPOTTING

Identify when repotting is necessary:

- Repot your fern when it becomes root-bound, with roots circling the container's bottom.
- Notice if the fern's growth is slowing down, indicating the need for fresh soil and more space.
- Consider repotting if the fern has outgrown its current container.

STEP 2: REPOTTING PROCESS

Follow these steps for repotting:

1. Gently remove the fern from its current container, being cautious not to damage the delicate roots.
2. Choose a new container that is slightly larger than the current one, with good drainage.
3. Place a layer of well-draining potting mix in the new container.
4. Position the fern in the center and fill the sides with more potting mix, gently firming it around the roots.
5. Water the fern thoroughly to settle the soil.

STEP 3: PROPAGATION METHODS

Explore different propagation methods:

- Division: Divide the fern by separating rhizomes with their own roots and fronds. Plant each division in a separate container.
- Offsets: Look for baby ferns (offsets) growing near the parent plant. Gently detach them and plant in their own containers.

STEP 4: PROPAGATION PROCESS

Follow these steps for propagation:

1. Identify suitable offsets or divisions with established roots.
2. Prepare small containers with well-draining potting mix.
3. Plant the offsets or divisions at the same depth they were previously growing.
4. Water the newly propagated plants gently and place them in appropriate lighting.

5. Maintain high humidity around the new plants to support their establishment.

STEP 5: NURTURING NEW GROWTH

Nurture the repotted and propagated plants:

- Place the repotted plant in suitable lighting conditions and adjust watering accordingly.
- Monitor the newly propagated plants for signs of growth and health.
- Continue regular care to ensure successful establishment and growth.

STEP 6: EXPANDING YOUR TERRARIUM

By repotting and propagating your Davallia (Rabbit's Foot Fern), you're expanding your open terrarium's beauty and diversity. The addition of new plants enhances the lushness of your miniature ecosystem and allows you to enjoy the captivating growth of multiple ferns within the same terrarium.

OPTIMIZING HUMIDITY LEVELS OF DAVALLIA (RABBIT'S FOOT FERN) IN YOUR OPEN TERRARIUM

Maintaining the right humidity levels in your open terrarium is essential for the health and well-being of your Davallia fern. Learn how to create an ideal humidity environment to ensure lush growth, prevent stress, and showcase the fern's beauty within your mini ecosystem.

STEP 1: UNDERSTANDING HUMIDITY NEEDS

Recognize the humidity requirements of your fern:

- Davallia ferns thrive in environments with higher humidity levels, mimicking their natural habitat.
- Adequate humidity promotes healthy frond development, prevents browning, and supports overall growth.
- Monitor humidity levels to prevent excessive dryness that can lead to stress and browning of the fern.

STEP 2: TERRARIUM PLACEMENT

Choose an appropriate location for the terrarium:

- Place the terrarium in a room with moderate to high humidity, such as a bathroom or near a humidifier.
- Avoid placing the terrarium in direct sunlight or near sources of dry heat, which can cause excessive evaporation.

STEP 3: PEBBLE TRAY

Use a pebble tray to increase humidity:

- Place a shallow tray filled with water and decorative pebbles near the terrarium.
- The water gradually evaporates, increasing the humidity around the fern without causing waterlogging.

STEP 4: MIST THE FERN

Mist the fern to elevate humidity:

- Spray the fronds and surrounding air with distilled water using a fine mist spray bottle.
- Misting helps maintain humidity levels and provides moisture directly to the fern's foliage.
- Avoid over-misting, as excessive moisture can lead to fungal issues.

STEP 5: MAINTAIN ADEQUATE VENTILATION

Balance humidity and ventilation:

- Ensure there's proper airflow within the terrarium to prevent excessive humidity buildup and potential mold growth.
- Monitor the terrarium's humidity and ventilation to strike the right balance for your fern's health.

STEP 6: THRIVING IN OPTIMAL HUMIDITY

By optimizing humidity levels, you're creating a thriving environment for your Davallia (Rabbit's Foot Fern) within your open terrarium. The balanced humidity not only enhances the fern's lushness but also showcases its beauty while contributing to a vibrant and healthy mini ecosystem.

LONG-TERM MAINTENANCE FOR DAVALLIA (RABBIT'S FOOT FERN): REPOTTING, REFRESHING, AND REJUVENATING YOUR OPEN TERRARIUM

Ensuring the long-term health and beauty of your Davallia fern in the open terrarium requires ongoing care and maintenance. Learn how to repot, refresh, and rejuvenate your terrarium to create a thriving and captivating miniature ecosystem that continues to enchant over time.

STEP 1: REPOTTING AND REASSESSMENT

Consider repotting as your fern grows:

- Monitor the fern's growth and assess if it has outgrown its current container.
- Repot the fern following the repotting steps to provide fresh soil and more space.
- Repotting rejuvenates the fern's root system and supports continued growth.

STEP 2: REFRESHING THE TERRARIUM

Refresh the terrarium's elements:

- Periodically rearrange decorative elements, rocks, and natural materials to keep the terrarium visually interesting.
- Prune and trim any overgrown fronds to maintain a balanced and well-proportioned appearance.
- Clean the terrarium's glass walls to ensure maximum visibility of the fern and its surroundings.

STEP 3: NUTRIENT BOOST

Provide a nutrient boost as needed:

- Consider top-dressing the soil with a thin layer of fresh potting mix to replenish nutrients.
- Apply diluted, balanced fertilizer to provide essential nutrients for continued growth.
- Regularly check the fern's foliage for signs of nutrient deficiency and adjust fertilization accordingly.

STEP 4: PREVENTIVE MEASURES

Prevent potential issues through vigilant care:

- Monitor humidity, light, and watering to prevent stress and keep the terrarium environment stable.
- Regularly inspect for signs of pests, diseases, or nutrient imbalances to address issues promptly.
- Implement preventive measures to ensure the terrarium remains a healthy and thriving ecosystem.

STEP 5: ONGOING ENJOYMENT

Continue to enjoy and admire your terrarium:

- Take time to observe the fern's growth, the evolving landscape, and the harmony of the miniature ecosystem.
- Adjust care routines based on the fern's changing needs and the terrarium's overall condition.
- Your ongoing attention and care will contribute to the enduring beauty of your Davallia fern and its open terrarium.

STEP 6: A TIMELESS DISPLAY

Long-term maintenance ensures that your Davallia (Rabbit's Foot Fern) open terrarium remains a timeless and captivating display of nature's wonders. Through repotting, refreshing, and rejuvenating, you'll continue to nurture an enchanting microcosm that brings beauty and tranquility to your space.

DESIGNING DAVALLIA (RABBIT'S FOOT FERN) IN YOUR OPEN TERRARIUM: CONSIDERING AESTHETICS AND ARRANGEMENT

Creating a visually appealing and harmonious arrangement in your open terrarium enhances the beauty of your Davallia fern and adds a touch of artistry to your miniature landscape. Learn how to design your terrarium with careful consideration of aesthetics and arrangement to create an enchanting and captivating display.

STEP 1: CHOOSE A FOCAL POINT

Select a central focal point:

- Choose a well-grown Davallia fern as the centerpiece of your terrarium.
- The focal point draws attention and sets the tone for the overall design.
- Position the fern slightly off-center to create a dynamic and balanced composition.

STEP 2: BALANCE AND PROPORTION

Achieve balance and proportion:

- Select complementary plants and decorative elements that harmonize with the fern's textures and colors.
- Avoid overcrowding and ensure each element has enough space to shine.
- Play with varying heights, shapes, and sizes for an engaging and visually pleasing arrangement.

STEP 3: LAYERING AND DEPTH

Create depth and layering:

- Arrange plants and materials in layers, with taller elements at the back and shorter ones towards the front.
- Use rocks, pebbles, and sand to add texture and depth to the terrarium's base.
- The layered arrangement gives the impression of a miniature landscape with visual depth.

STEP 4: CONTRAST AND COLOR

Utilize contrast and color:

- Pair different shades of green and other colors to create contrast and visual interest.
- Consider using colorful pebbles, rocks, or decorative elements that complement the fern's foliage.
- Use color strategically to guide the viewer's eye and create focal points within the terrarium.

STEP 5: NATURAL ELEMENTS

Incorporate natural elements:

- Add miniature figurines, small rocks, driftwood, or other natural items to enhance the terrarium's charm.
- These elements contribute to the story and theme of your miniature ecosystem.
- Place natural elements thoughtfully to enhance the overall design without overwhelming the fern.

STEP 6: PERSONAL TOUCH

Infuse your personality:

- Create a design that resonates with your style and preferences, whether it's minimalistic, whimsical, or artistic.
- Allow your terrarium to be a reflection of your creativity and imagination.
- Your personal touch adds a unique and meaningful dimension to the design.

STEP 7: AESTHETIC DELIGHT

By thoughtfully designing your Davallia (Rabbit's Foot Fern) open terrarium, you're creating an aesthetic delight that captivates the eye and sparks joy. The arrangement becomes more than just a collection of plants—it's a work of art that brings beauty and tranquility to your space.

ENHANCING YOUR TERRARIUM WITH DECORATIVE ELEMENTS FOR DAVALLIA (RABBIT'S FOOT FERN): ADDING VISUAL INTEREST AND CREATIVITY

Infusing your Davallia fern terrarium with decorative elements elevates its aesthetic appeal and lets your creativity shine. Learn how to introduce decorative elements to your terrarium to create a captivating and personalized miniature world that reflects your style and imagination.

STEP 1: THEME AND STORY

Develop a theme or story for your terrarium:

- Choose a theme that resonates with you, such as a mystical forest, a tranquil oasis, or a fairy garden.
- The theme guides your choice of decorative elements and creates a cohesive narrative.
- Think about the story you want your terrarium to tell and how decorative items can contribute to it.

STEP 2: MINIATURE FIGURINES

Add miniature figurines:

- Select tiny figurines that match your chosen theme, such as animals, fairies, or fantasy creatures.
- Place figurines strategically to create scenes and interactions within the terrarium.
- Figurines bring a sense of whimsy and enchantment to your miniature world.

STEP 3: DECORATIVE ROCKS AND PEBBLES

Incorporate decorative rocks and pebbles:

- Choose colorful or uniquely shaped rocks and pebbles to add texture and visual interest.
- Arrange them to create pathways, borders, or natural formations within the terrarium.
- Decorative rocks enhance the terrarium's landscape and contribute to its overall aesthetics.

STEP 4: DRIFTWOOD AND TWIGS

Introduce driftwood and twigs:

- Use small pieces of driftwood or twigs to mimic trees, logs, or natural structures.
- Position them to create height variation and simulate a more diverse environment.
- Driftwood and twigs add a touch of authenticity and charm to the terrarium.

STEP 5: PERSONALIZED TOUCHES

Infuse personalized touches:

- Add personal items like tiny trinkets, seashells, or miniature objects that hold significance to you.
- These items make your terrarium unique and reflect your personality and memories.
- Personalized touches create a special connection with your miniature world.

STEP 6: EXPRESSIVE CREATIVITY

By enhancing your Davallia (Rabbit's Foot Fern) terrarium with decorative elements, you're expressing your creativity and making the miniature ecosystem truly your own. The carefully chosen figurines, rocks, and personal items contribute to the enchanting story of your terrarium, inviting admiration and sparking curiosity.

DESIGNING MINIATURE GARDENS FOR DAVALLIA (RABBIT'S FOOT FERN): CONSTRUCTING MINIATURE LANDSCAPES IN YOUR TERRARIUM

Creating miniature gardens within your Davallia fern terrarium allows you to craft enchanting and captivating landscapes on a small scale. Learn how to design and construct miniature landscapes using various elements, textures, and plants to transport you into a world of whimsy and beauty.

STEP 1: CHOOSE A LANDSCAPE THEME

Select a theme for your miniature landscape:

- Opt for themes such as a lush forest, a serene meadow, a coastal scene, or a rocky mountain landscape.
- The chosen theme guides your plant selection and design elements.
- Consider the atmosphere and story you want to evoke with your miniature garden.

STEP 2: LAYERING AND TERRAIN

Create layers and varying terrain:

- Use materials like potting mix, sand, and pebbles to simulate different terrains such as hills, valleys, and shorelines.
- Layer the materials strategically to form natural contours and elevations.
- The terrain creates visual interest and adds depth to your miniature landscape.

STEP 3: PLANT SELECTION

Choose plants that fit the landscape theme:

- Select plants with diverse textures, heights, and colors to mimic the flora of your chosen landscape.
- Use the Davallia fern as a central element and complement it with other miniature plants.
- The plants should evoke the essence of the chosen landscape and contribute to the overall design.

STEP 4: DECORATIVE ELEMENTS

Add decorative elements for realism:

- Incorporate miniature figurines, rocks, and natural materials like twigs to enhance the landscape's authenticity.
- Use decorative elements to create scenes, pathways, and natural formations within the miniature garden.
- Each element contributes to the story and character of your landscape.

STEP 5: VISUAL BALANCE AND COMPOSITION

Achieve visual balance and composition:

- Distribute plants and elements evenly to create a harmonious and pleasing arrangement.
- Consider the placement of focal points, pathways, and areas of interest within the miniature landscape.
- The visual composition guides the viewer's eye and tells a captivating story.

STEP 6: CREATIVE EXPRESSION

Designing miniature gardens within your Davallia (Rabbit's Foot Fern) terrarium is a form of creative expression that transports you into a world of imagination. As you construct intricate landscapes, you're crafting a tiny realm that invites you to explore its beauty and intricacies, evoking wonder and fascination.

USING DRIFTWOOD AND BRANCHES FOR DAVALLIA (RABBIT'S FOOT FERN): CREATING NATURAL HABITATS WITHIN THE TERRARIUM

Incorporating driftwood and branches in your Davallia fern terrarium adds a touch of authenticity and creates natural habitats for your plants. Learn how to use these elements to simulate trees, logs, and natural structures, enriching your miniature ecosystem with a sense of realism and harmony.

STEP 1: SELECTION AND PREPARATION

Choose driftwood and branches thoughtfully:

- Select pieces that fit the scale of your terrarium and complement the fern's size and aesthetics.
- Collect driftwood and branches from safe and sustainable sources, or purchase them from reputable sources.
- Clean and sanitize the pieces to remove dirt, debris, and potential contaminants before placing them in the terrarium.

STEP 2: CREATING HEIGHT VARIATION

Use driftwood and branches to add height:

- Position taller pieces towards the back of the terrarium to create depth and height variation.
- Simulate the appearance of trees or shrubs by arranging branches in a way that mimics their growth patterns.
- The varying heights provide visual interest and contribute to a more dynamic terrarium landscape.

STEP 3: SIMULATING NATURAL STRUCTURES

Mimic natural structures with driftwood and branches:

- Arrange driftwood to resemble fallen logs, fallen trees, or natural structures you'd find in a forest or woodland setting.
- Use smaller branches to create natural pathways or simulate fallen branches on the forest floor.
- The natural structures add a sense of realism and create microhabitats within the terrarium.

STEP 4: MOSS AND EPIPHYTES

Enhance driftwood and branches with moss and epiphytes:

- Attach mosses, small ferns, and epiphytic plants to the driftwood and branches using non-toxic glue or wire.

- The plants grow on these surfaces just as they would in nature, further enhancing the natural appearance.
- Mosses and epiphytes contribute to the overall aesthetic and provide additional habitat for the terrarium's inhabitants.

STEP 5: AUTHENTICITY AND CHARM

Using driftwood and branches in your Davallia (Rabbit's Foot Fern) terrarium brings authenticity and charm to your miniature world. These natural elements not only enhance the aesthetics but also create intricate habitats that mirror the beauty of forests and woodlands, providing a unique and captivating experience for both you and your fern.

CONCLUSION: DAVALLIA (RABBIT'S FOOT FERN) IN TERRARIUM

Cultivating the Davallia (Rabbit's Foot Fern) within a terrarium offers an opportunity to create a captivating microcosm that combines nature's beauty with your creativity. Throughout this guide, you've explored the art and science of nurturing a thriving ecosystem within the confines of glass walls. From understanding the fern's needs to designing landscapes and selecting complementary elements, you've embarked on a journey of crafting a harmonious world in miniature.

HARMONY OF NATURE AND ARTISTRY

The terrarium becomes a canvas:

- Your Davallia fern flourishes within its carefully designed environment, showcasing its intricate fronds and vibrant growth.
- The combination of soil, substrate, decorative elements, and design choices brings together a harmonious microcosm that reflects your vision.
- Through your artistry, you've sculpted a piece of nature that's both beautiful and intimate.

ENDLESS EXPLORATION

Your journey continues:

- As your terrarium evolves, you'll witness the fern's growth, the transformation of landscapes, and the stories of its inhabitants.
- Adapting care techniques, refreshing designs, and responding to seasonal changes will be part of the ongoing adventure.
- Your Davallia fern terrarium becomes a dynamic tableau that offers endless exploration and creativity.

A SLICE OF TRANQUILITY

A serene oasis in your space:

- As you admire your Davallia fern's lush fronds, the miniature landscapes, and the artful arrangement, you'll find a slice of tranquility and connection to nature.
- Your terrarium invites contemplation, wonder, and a moment of respite from the world outside.
- Through its beauty and your care, the terrarium becomes a source of joy and a testament to your dedication.

A LIVING WORK OF ART

Ultimately, your Davallia (Rabbit's Foot Fern) terrarium transcends being a mere container of plants; it becomes a living work of art that intertwines the elegance of nature with your creativity. With each thoughtful choice, every nurturing gesture, and every glimpse of its thriving existence, you're part of a captivating story that celebrates life's beauty in its most intricate and diminutive form.

Made in United States
Orlando, FL
17 March 2024